About the Author

Prophetesstara.com

Tara Walker Smith is a daughter, wife, mother, and prophet of God sent forth to break the chains, heal & bring forth deliverance in the name of Jesus Christ!

She is a testimony to many that grace abounds! Being birth through a cancerous womb not expected to live; God's hands of protection have been upon her from the beginning.

With a multifaceted anointing, yielded heart, and her Yes to the Lord; she goes forth to prophesy and preach the Gospel of Jesus Christ. .

God has given her a word of life, hope, deliverance, and restoration. One soul at a Time she has vowed to provoke the hearts of man to turn to God! Everywhere she goes, she proclaims that Jesus is Lord & WITH GOD ALL THINGS ARE POSSIBLE!!!!!

Table of contents

Dedication

"As iron sharpens iron, so one person sharpens another." Proverbs 27:17

This book is dedicated to ones who have been a great inspiration to me. Their names are Bonnie Walker, Joyce Sims, Tammy Bradford Gadson, Sheila and Ricky Floyd, Kelly Crews, Manuel and Tanika Mukes, Rod and Taketa Williams, Everett and Lou Ann Heidelberg.

To: Bonnie Walker- *My mother and my friend, you have been one of my greatest support to accomplishing the things that the Lord has called me to do. Thanks for your willingness to go the extra mile to make things happen with me. You have given me life! I still say "I'm your greatest blessing!" (Smile)*

To: Joyce Sims- *Thanks for being an example of what happens when a person gives God what he requires. I can remember your heart towards giving God what is due His name growing up. What you've shown me has become foundation to my obedience towards Him. Thanks for being that for me.*

To: Apostle Tammy Gadson, *my sister, my friend, thanks for always listening and pushing me to move forward with the plans of God. It's amazing to me still how much we are alike in spirit! Your willingness to go that extra mile with me, I am forever grateful!*

"A Prophet's Little Book of Wisdom"

To: Pastors Sheila and Ricky Floyd, *from the moment I met you until now you have proven to walk in nothing but excellence and integrity! You all came into my life and helped to restore how I saw leadership! You've shown nothing but love to me. Thanks for pushing me to be who I am called to be. The wisdom that you so easily poured into me I will not forget! I have gleaned so much by watching you and your walk has proven to be consistent with your talk! Thanks for that!*

To: Prophetess Kelly Crews, *I don't know where to begin, I will say thanks for your willingness to do what no one else has in my life (complete my assignment)! Your eagerness to see me win and efforts to make it happen has been an extreme blessing to me! All the calls and texts that always seem to come at the right time. I can only say, "Whew, I thank God for this divine connection!"*

To: Pastors Manuel and Tanika Mukes, *Oh my God you are to me an example of freedom! You've shown me through your walk alone the definition of remaining authentic and the benefits that comes from it. The wisdom that you've given me I will never forget. You are walking with power! Warriors standing on the wall! Thanks for sounding the alarms and giving me instructions on what to do next!*

To: Apostle Rod and Prophetess Taketa Williams, *I often say, you know how to start a fire, blow up the scene, and then just like that YOU'RE OUT! Just as fast as you show up; you wreck the place and vroom you are gone! Apostle Rod you are one of the greatest teachers I have heard in my life. You are MOST DEFINITELY A QUIET STORM.*

Thanks for the many things you've allowed me to see through your transparency. I've often looked for an example of something that kind of looks like what God has given me. My husband and I are called to ministry together. I am no way that quiet sit on chair and keep quiet type of 1ˢᵗ lady.

You came into our lives when we were broken in so many places. I won't ever forget how you helped to put those things together again.

Jason always says "Tara we are kindred to the Williams." So thanks for giving me hope! We know covering is very important and I believe you should be covered. Nonetheless, your covering should resemble you according to who you are and where you are going. Thanks for giving me hope!

To: Prophetess Lou Ann and Apostle Everett Heidelberg, *last but certainly not least. I just to say thank you for those foundational things that you have poured into me. I can often hear you guys saying "Dorothy you are a long way from home! We're not in Kansas anymore Toto!" The wisdom I have learned under your tutelage I can apply on many levels of life and ministry. Thanks so much!*

You all have influenced my life for better in an extreme way. I have watched you and through your lifestyle I've gleaned greatness. What I have obtained from you has brought solidity to my foundation. Thanks for the many things that you've poured into me.

"A Prophet's Little Book of Wisdom"

May the Lord honor you for your obedience and willingness to foster the enormity that he is birthing forth in the Earth! You've been an asset to the woman of God that I am yet becoming. Thanks for your eagerness to give and to love.
You are appreciated!

Tara Walker Smith

FOREWORD

Upon meeting Prophetess Tara Walker Smith I was immediately drawn to the fact that she was full of many nuggets. Whenever I would ask a question, she provided an answer that would always make me say "Wow, that's good." What I loved the most was that I knew she was not only providing wisdom and counsel but Godly wisdom and Godly counsel (and believe me there is a difference). In this hour when there is so much information available from so many different sources, it is truly refreshing to receive wisdom from a mighty woman of God who is both humble and transparent all at the same time. It's even better because not only do I call her Prophetess but I have had the awesome privilege to call her friend.

The word "nugget" is defined as **a** lump, esp. of native gold or other precious metal. Anything small but of great value or significance: *nuggets of wisdom.*

When you read "A Prophet's Little Book of Wisdom", you quickly begin to realize that you have obtained a book that is packed with power, precious in God's sight, and full of significant nuggets of Godly wisdom. The lessons taught are literally lifted from the pages of Prophetess Tara's life and ministry, which means you, can expect every chapter to be real, raw, and life changing.

In one example in the second chapter she deals with a subject near and dear to my heart and something that many of you will be able to relate to: approval, rejection and acceptance by man vs. doing and being exactly who God has called you and created you to be.

As you know, most people live their lives for others. We live for someone else's approval, confirmation, and affirmation. This begins at birth and many times stays with us through the rest of our lives. In her words, "We spend time chasing people who don't care to be caught. Time after time through their actions, they have shown us who they are, their passion toward what we are doing, and their devotion towards us. Yet we are constantly trying to convince them that what we are sensing is real and we are going to do great things. At best they read the memo and keep moving." How many times have you "chased" someone or something that was not to be "caught"? As I read this, I immediately felt a quickening in my mind and spirit.

Propelling, Purposeful, Passionate - are the three words I would use to describe "A Prophet's Little Book of Wisdom", God has allowed Prophetess Tara to speak words where you will feel not only truth but that her words are a much needed balm to many hurt and wounded souls. Be prepared to take off the mask of religion and routine. Be prepared to receive insight and revelation. Be prepared to walk away from reading this book with a renewed mind, a renewed motivation, and a renewed might to do what God called you to do!

Apostle Tammy Bradford-Gadson, San Antonio, TX
Pastor of Free Worship Deliverance Ministries
www.freeworshipdeliveranceministries.com

Introduction

Life has a way of throwing things at us that we can't understand. Many times, we are faced with challenges that seem to appear out of nowhere. In this book, I've decided to describe a few things I've had to endure as a prophet and the wisdom I've obtained throughout the process.

I am mindful that everything about a prophet's life is prophetic. We have to walk alongside of God and man. When concerning the matters of His heart, God often uses of us as His mouthpiece to speak His mind to others.

We are first partakers of the voice of God that activates movement in the Earth. Anything we experience is never JUST for us. Realizing that, I know that I am sent to grasp those who have been ordained by God since the beginning of all creations for me to reach. I am here for people filled with purpose! Ultimately, that purpose is to bring glory, honor, and dominion back to him.

"A Prophet's Little Book of Wisdom"

A Prophet's Little Book of Wisdom is just that, a book comprised of situations that different people may face and don't know how to move forward from it. Lord knows I've had to experience some things that I wish someone could have warned me about.

If you can relate to what I'm writing, there are applicable keys that will bring forth positive results in your life. I hope that through my writings, you are empowered to be a better you and never settle for less than you desire. These are testimonies of the things I've battled through and how God strategically brought me out.

I pray that something written in this book will inspire you to seek Him for the best and outstanding things in your life. You are worth it! Any investment in your life will bring forth the security of a lifetime.

Chapter I
"Lord Help Me"

Where there is no closure to a relationship, we find a way to hang on even if there is no inkling of life. Why is that? We find ourselves left in lingo because we want to believe the best in them and they will change. Of course, this only leads us to waste weeks, months, or years of our lives. Life is too precious to be waiting on people and hanging on to the possibility of what they could be.

For example: we may have been in a relationship with someone and recently broken up with them. It's never a good idea to jump right into another relationship with another person. We need time to heal and to bounce back from the prior relationship before moving into something else. Surely we don't want to take baggage with us (such as unresolved issues) into another relationship. Why make someone else pay for what you are currently walking your way through?

Nonetheless, we find ways to cope with not having that special someone in our lives. Initially, it's going to be hard to get over unless you had absolutely no feelings for the person.

Let's suppose that there are some unresolved issues and there weren't closure. You know for women, we have certain questions we desire to have answered before we consider it to be over. If not, we are left in a place and finding it hard to move forward from. We have to at least have an understanding on where we are (as it relates to over and no communication or over and friends.), why it didn't work, and etc. These questions will vary contingent on the nature of the break-up and woman.

Nevertheless, we "try" to move forward and if these questions aren't answered or we don't get proper closure we will find ourselves hanging on to something that has died or God is trying to kill. So we end up spending time waiting to see if the relationship can be restored. We wait to see, if that person is willing to have any dealing with us after the cool down period. Sadly, those who we are waiting for have moved on with their lives.

Nonetheless, there has been improper closure and we are putting our lives on hold. When memories of what have transpired through the duration the relationship bombards our minds and it's hard to think soberly. If we don't maintain or take control it cripples us and surfaces all types of emotions.

When this is your doings let me warn you of a few things. One: while waiting for them, you are probably missing some great opportunities of meeting some wonderful people. If it was a bitter break up, learn how to forgive them. Don't allow those images to play over and over in your head. When you allow the images to replay that only sets you up to be harsh in your dealing with others.

Two: Don't be that "go too" person! Don't be the one that your ex comes to when they are bored or need some action. We make the mistake of thinking if we allow them to come into our lives when it's convenient for them, they will see our love for them. So we will settle with having a piece of them rather than being without them completely. If they aren't willing to commit in the relationship totally to you and only you, choose to end it completely. If not you will be that "go to"

person that they find when they can't be
with the one they really desire.

Three: A: Don't put your life on hold. Yes,
we should always see the best in others.
There lives should also be aligning
accordingly. I mean, at least keep them
accountable. Don't just believe that they will
become what you see without holding them
conscientious for pursuing their goals.

B: If you are with someone like this push
them to make good on what they have said
or you will be setting yourself up. In other
words, you can't keep expecting them to be
a doctor and they haven't even registered for
school. How long do they sit on the couch
before you decide what you see (in the
spirit) is not aligning in the natural with
what you see.

Ask yourself, I am willing to wait this out?
Are they making valid efforts to see their
dreams come to pass? Ultimately, it's up to
the person to pursue it but at least you are
doing your best to be an asset. Don't cripple
them more by accepting the mediocre.

Truth is the longer we spend waiting,
wishing, and hoping; we could be spending
maximize the times and the moment that are

before us. We should never give that much power over to someone to control our movements. It's controlled through the illusions of this perfect life that we create of them being with us in a particular way, form, or fashion in our minds. Not that we shouldn't envision our lives in a state brighter than the one set before us (because there are times God will reveal a thing to us), just remain grounded.

When what we perceive to be truth takes a toll on how we are functioning in our day to day activities we need to regroup, strategize and start over. You deserve better! Pursue it!!!!!

Chapter II
"Turn Around- It's already done"

It's funny how we spend our whole lives waiting for manifestations of blessings that God has already delivered to us. For example: We pray about having our "loved ones" supporting us in our endeavors. We spend our time trying to get them to see what God has shown us, the dream that we've envisioned, and how it's for everyone. We do so while neglecting those who He sends as an answer to our prayers.

We spend time chasing people who don't care to be caught. Through their actions, they have shown us who they are, their passion toward what we are doing, and their devotion towards us. We are constantly trying to convince them that what we are sensing is real and we are going to do great things. At best, they read the memo and keep moving.

Nevertheless, there's something that keeps motivating us to pursue what we see. In spite of the lack of sustenance, we fight to continue. We pick up the pieces of not being supported by those who matter the most and make things happen. We do so with a struggle because they never take time to acknowledge our accomplishments (and if their support is what we desire the most); it only leads to greater hurt and frustrations. If we are not careful, this will move us into a cycle.

We then move from a place of being excited about what God has shown and graced us to accomplish into a place of performing for the applauds of man. I've learned that we spend too much time trying to prove that we are who God says we are. In doing so, we lose the essence of who we are created to be. Chasing a person who doesn't care to be caught by us only takes us farther off course. Break the cycle and stay the course!

Since God has given us this great dream and vision, we should pour all of our effort, time, and resources into what He has graced us with. Once we begin to do this, we will look around and find those "loved ones" who we desire support from walking with us. There will also be ones added to us through the divine connections that he has strategically placed in our lives.

Keep in mind the story that occurs in Matthew chapter 25 about the oil. It's wise to use the oil on what it is for. Do not burn your oil on things that are irrelevant. When we make the decision to chase after people to support us; IT BURNS OUR OIL. It's a tactic that the enemy uses to distract us and make nasty deposits in our hearts. It has the same effect that rejections have upon us.

When we are rejected adjustments MUST be made or it will choke out our creativity, blind us from seeing things as God sees, and it will cause us to burn a lot of our time (oil).

Rejection is never easy to deal with when it comes from our spouse, family, friends, and those you want to make a great impact on. Have you noticed? The more you chase them the more they run. Stop and give God the opportunity to show you another way. God's will for our lives is perfect and he is orchestrating our destiny. Those who our dreams will impact the most we won't have to chase or convince them of who we are; they will ABSOLUTELY know.

Take time to refocus on what is important. Maximize all that God as placed on the inside of you by believing and pursuing it.

God has people who were created just for you. They are drawn to you and the very essences of who you are created to be. They know what they need is on the inside of you. They are thirsty for it with passion.

Be encouraged! You are everything you see and God says you are. Don't allow the trickery of distractions that the enemy sends to frustrate you from becoming all that you have envisioned.

Chapter III
"My Big Mouth"

Often times when we are angry, we speak things that we shouldn't. We fail to tame our tongues.

For it is written: *"but no human being can tame the tongue. It is a restless evil, full of deadly poison." James 3:8.*

Through frustrations, we release toxic words that are usually never reversed. As a result, what we speak lingers in our atmosphere, manifests, and helps to create the world we live in.

For example, we have spats. From those quarrels, we say what we aren't and are going to do and how awful it was what "they" have done toward us. We paint a pretty picture of ourselves while leaving a picture of debacle towards others.

By doing this we make travesty of who we are and everything we stand for. It's likely after we are calmer; we have the ability to see things clearer. God will begin to purge our hearts. The Lord through those encounters speaks and we are healed.

No doubt when this happens, forgiveness easily transpires.

Isn't that like God? Soon after He deals with us; we find ourselves doing most of the things we said we weren't going to do. The sad part is by the time we've reconciled (with the ones we had the spat with), ones (we took our issues too) couldn't handle it. Hinged upon their nature, we have caused more damage than good. You know it's the truth!

We have spent all night talking to whoever will listen to us. While ranting, we say, "We are through with someone." "They have done us wrong for the last time." Then, we talk to the Lord and He speaks, "Forgive them and continue in relations!"

I mean, if you have ever had one of these moments then you know what I am talking about. It's like a punch in the chest. You are like "Lord! Do you not see what just happened?" Trust me, He immediately shows you how He sees it and HOW HE SEES YOU! It's nothing like we've perceived it to be. After He has finished telling you about yourself, forgiving them is no longer an issue (Smile).

Now reality sets in and we have to face those who we talked to about our situation. Those who we talked to (about ones we had the spats with) are wondering why we went back? Why did we do the opposite of what we said? Many will deem us as hypocritical.

These same ones will begin to question our ethics. They look at us like we are cowards. The truth is: The ones we confided in only had one part of the story. The part they had wasn't meant for them. Through our immaturity, we involved them instead going strong to the Lord in prayer.

The mystery of it all is through our actions, we have launched a chain of events. Now we are all positioned in a place of testing. We are being observed by the Lord on how we handled things. It would have been proper for us to bring those things to him in prayer and leave them there. It would have been proper for them to discern our words, intercede for us, and to refrain from being judgmental.

For it is written: *"And "don't sin by letting anger control you." Don't let the sun go down while you are still angry, Ephesians 4:26(NLT)*

God desires for us to remain sinless. He is dedicated to bringing out the best in us. That's evident in the working of the Cross of Jesus Christ.

The Cross was a vehicle to get Jesus to a greater place of glory. This remains true for us even today. Through Jesus we obtain grace to handle all situations that we may face. In Him, we find the strategies to win in our daily challenges. Therefore, the same grace that is available to us after we sin is available to keep us from sinning.

Love is so powerful. It covers a multitude of wrongs. For it is written: *"Above all, keep loving one another earnestly, since love covers a multitude of sins" I Peter 4:8.* The Lord urges us to continue to sow a labor of love and to ask him for wisdom.

As we genuinely seek the Lord in those perplexing times, He draws us closer to Him. We are governed by the measure of pursuit in us towards God.

It's the source for rivers of intimacy being open through worship. We are renewed in His presence. We obtain through our encounters just what we need. See initially we may go to Him upset. After we have talked to the Lord, He has a way of shedding a new light on the situation. It's never what it looks like.

After He speaks to us, we began to shift. We walk out of his presence with an inner peace that's unexplainable. Nonetheless, this takes discipline to do with consistency. It is also very rewarding.

The more we choose to handle our difficulties in the face of God; the wiser we become. He releases practical instructions that will enable us to be immovable in any or all situations. I'm telling you, when things arise you will find yourselves running to the safety of the Lord. Once in His presence, you will be able to quickly release and forgive those who you are engaged in misunderstandings with.

We must always be willing to make necessary adjustments to finish our assignments (in the righteousness of God). Remember the reason we are connected to people is to bring us into a grander place of purpose. So be disciplined in your walk to bring splendor and honor to Him (especially in times of difficulty). He will bless you for it!

Chapter IV
"Don't let Control…Control You"

On occasion, we come across people who have control issues. Usually the grip of their control extends with selfish demands driven by egotistical ambitions. On the contrary, what they are willing to give to you by no means is an even exchange.

Their expectations from you are held at premier regards but at best they will only reciprocate effortless deposits. They desire that you support them in all that they do. Lord forbids if you refuse to be a part of their program, there are gruesome ramifications to pay.

Once you find yourself in dealing with people like this, many signs and warnings are released through your interactions. PAY ATTENTION!!!

For example: one of the control mechanisms is to build walls of culmination. They desire to "close you out". They will purposely distance themselves from you in order to get your attention. It's their good pleasure to send you message of "get with the program or get gone". This tactic is a sure sign that they are annoyed with the fact that you haven't submitted to their demands. They are displeased with you and at this point will go to great lengths to show it.

Silent treatment, withholding vital information and a show of disapproval comes along with the territory. These types of people as long as you are doing what they require of you all is well. You must be a yes "man", anything outside of that you are not supportive; you are in opposition to what the "Lord" desires.

If you are on duty, during this time, they will purposely try to make wrapping up and completing your assignment difficult. Whatever you do don't abort but make sure you attune to the Lord and finish it.

Beware these types will go to great lengths to get out of us what they aspire. Even if that means bewitching us with lies and strings of deception, they will do it. They are not concerned with the method of trickery that they use. Their overall agenda is to draw us under their control by any means necessary.

When dealing with these types its best do only what the Lord says and remove yourself. Occasionally, it's hard to complete your obligation because their demands on you will conflict with the Lord's instructions. Make sure that you don't turn from what God has initiated you to do.

If you happen to turn, they will lead you off path. You will find yourself in a web of defeat. Demands will constantly be given that leads to more flesh gratification.

Since you moved from the Lord's original plan and allowed them to lead you off course, you will regret it. Due to your disobedience in this place, God is silent. Even when you pray, nothing happens. The only way out is through your obedience. So it's best to stay on the path provided by the Lord and run the race EXACTLY THE WAY HE GIVES IT TO YOU!

Chapter V

"Never dumb down….Be you"

Never dumb down whom you are in order to be engrafted in another person's world. God has fashioned you to be you. You are unique and built with purpose in mind. Just think of all the people you have come across along the way. So let's say it's been a few hundred, thousand, tens of thousands you have encountered.

The ones who stick out the most are those who have made the greatest impacts (whether good or bad). Trust me there are ones you won't care to remember but by the nature of the happenstance you will. For an example: I can remember getting into a fight with a young lady when I was on the bus at a youth. I really don't remember her name but I remember that encounter.

Can you imagine coming into company of people and never fulfilling your assignments? While you are in their company, because of your uncertainties about yourself, you can never be you. Maybe you have battled with thoughts that have you caged in. "What if they don't like me? What if they don't accept me?" So what? You still have the responsibility to remain who the Lord has ordained you to be.

If you have to dumb yourself down to make a good impression on man usually, you've made a bad impact on God. So never ever dumb yourself down. A little leak of you here and a little there it won't be long before you can't recognize who you are. Nobody is worth that.

I can tell you it's not fun, losing grips of who you are to please people. You make all these changes to keep them in your life. Because they have become your idol, God decides to remove them. What you've done profits nothing. It's an overwhelming feeling of ineptness when you've sacrificed the best of you and they still walk out of your life.

If this book finds you in a place where you have dumb yourself down, daily begin to call yourself back into the right place with the Lord. It starts through repentance. Go to God in prayer asking Him to show you who He has formed you to be. You owe it to yourself to be the best you- you can be.

There is so much potential in you. The problem is you have surrounded yourself around people who you aren't called too. It's almost like connecting yourself to a power source that drains you of your ability to shine. Begin to position yourself around people who will edify you and build you up. These are ones that are so secure in themselves that they promote you being you. I have met quite a few in my lifetime! (Smile)

Let the light that has been hid for so long shine through. I mean, the real you! Those who absolutely adore you are waiting for you to show up! Due to the fact that it's been masked they have found it hard to distinguish you from all others. Rise up and shine the whole world waits for the unveiling of the factual you!

Chapter VI
"Chosen beyond Appearances"

In this society we live in, we often times have heard the statement: It's not always what you know but it's who you know. I'm sure you have seen mortal men play the favorites.

These type look beyond a person's potential, experience, and qualifications (the lack thereof) and extend favors due to the person they may know who is related to such ones. They go by if the person is going to be reliable, a great worker and etc based solemnly upon their relationship person's family member or friend or a family's name. Not saying I disagree or agree, I am just merely stating the facts.

God on the other hand in His SOVERIEGNTY looks beyond such things and looks at the heart of man. He has a way of finding the less likely person (in man's eye) and increases value. Once God has placed His stamp of approval upon us, it doesn't matter who we may know.

In Samuel's case, in the beginning of his call, He had absolutely no relationship with the Lord. God saw and knew who he would be long before Samuel had known for Himself. We all remember how David was the less likely candidate in his father's entire house, yet God chose him.

The facts remain true today. We can see this being implemented in our lives. Some of us have backgrounds of malice, disobedience towards God, and living life in the safe zone. Whatever the case maybe, before God, we were all lost.

Even in the midst of being lost and out of place HE CHOSE US. For it is written: "Then Peter opened his mouth, and said, of a truth I perceive that God is no respecter of persons" Acts 10:34

I said all of that to say, what God is doing in your life, He will manifest. We make the mistake of thinking "man" will put us on or give us these grand opportunities. By doing so, we give them too much power over the will of God for our lives. Nothing happens for us without the permission of the Lord. It's through His divine will that we prosper and become who we aspire to be.

Once we are in sync with Him; He makes it all happen. So don't give up your "Birth

Right" being hungry for it to manifest in a hurry. Wait on God. Don't Compromise! Man recognizes our zeal to do what we've envisioned ourselves doing.

Along with our zeal often comes impatience. When we are impatient, it robs us of making sober decisions. Bam! Before we know it, they have negotiated us right out of what the Lord has promised us. Our blessings are to be cherished, guarded, and held in greater significance. We should never worship the blessings because WORSHIP BELONGS TO GOD. We are to appreciate it. Never waste or give up your promise for a temporary fulfillment. Once you've lost it, it's hard to get back!!!!!

Chapter VII
"Assassin to Honor"

When people become familiar with us it obstructs how effective we flow in their lives. It's not that we are incompetent of fulfilling the task. They lack giving the honor necessary to see it manifested in their lives.

For it is written: Then Jesus told them, "A prophet is honored everywhere except in his own hometown and among his relatives and his own family" Mark6:4. It wasn't because of insufficiencies in the prophet but it was because of how the people viewed them. Even today, it's common in our lives.

You know how we try to help those who are close to us. They say through their actions "That's just Tara or Cousin Bananas." Can anything good come from them? For it is written in John 1:46 "Nazareth!" exclaimed Nathanael. "Can anything good come from Nazareth?"

You too may have encountered those who say, is there anything good that can come from that family, person, bloodline, and etc. We should always take note from Jesus.

He did what He could and took the best of Him to areas in which He was received. We should never take it personal but learn to maintain focus. Our focus on God is essential for completion of the assignment.

I can remember ministering to someone who knows me. I saw that a spirit of suicide was waiting to catch them off guard. God revealed to me, it came through a door that they had opened. I gave specific instructions in order for them to see deliverance. Nevertheless, they didn't heed to the instructions and battled with that spirit for days afterward. The next time I saw them they were willing to succumb God's instruction and they received deliverance.

Warfare and routing out demons are nothing new to me. God has utilized me to do so on several occasions. On another occasion, I begin to minister to another person I know personally. With deliverance sometimes, it's a process and it takes tarrying to uproot completely.

The first time I ministered to this person, I sensed the person who I was assisting fighting against me as well. It wasn't that God hadn't permitted that person's time of

35

breakthrough but they just had an issue with the Lord using me to do so.

So the more I begin to minister deliverance; they would quench it. There are times when demonic spirits (doorkeepers) will try to prevent deliverance from going forth. This time was different than those types of encounters; the person who I was ministering to was stubbornly trying to block it.

They didn't yield to the instructions of the Lord that I was giving them. They were trying to get it another way. I ended up stopping in the process until they were ready to receive what the Lord was doing. These are the type that no matter how much you minister it just flows back to you. I mean, you can feel it literally. These are ones I deemed closed vessels.

Later on that night, I received a phone call from them. They've had an encounter with those demonic spirits. I was limited to what I could do because even after that encounter; they STILL were not willing to submit to the instructions and leading of the Lord that flowed through me. There are times when honor controls the flow of the prophet. This was one of those times.

When you have a genuine desire to see your loved ones and those who know you receive deliverance and breakthrough; it's hard to walk away. It's like you watch them go through a season of defeat (when it could have been avoided). Often times, God will give them over to you for breakthrough but what can you do when there is no honor? What can you do, when they allow how they see you to hinder what God is bringing forth through you?

The best thing to do is sow the seeds into the lives of those who receive you. AGAIN I SAY, Don't take it personal! Be sure to remain in expectation that what you have sown in the lives of others you will reap in the lives of your loved ones.

Now this should never be your motivation but it can easily help to fuel the passion to obey the Lord. Remember when we are WILLING and OBEDIENT, we will eat the good of the Land!!! I receive it and decree it so in every area of our lives in Jesus name, Amen!

Chapter VIII
"Breaking Bars of Imprisonment"
(Insecurity)

God has invested so much in us. We were created in His image with endless possibilities. Security is one of the least things God's children should struggle with, but we do. Insecurity is defined as not being self-confident; subject to fears.

When a person walks in insecurity it builds bars of imprisonment around them and everything they have stewardship over. Its root stems from a lack of confidence.

Usually those who are insecure also struggle with fear. Fear paralyzes them to the point they are afraid to step out on what God has shown them. They live a life of limitations. Excuses, procrastinations, sabotage, anger, and are a part of the lifestyle for these types. It just depends on what level of insecurity has ensnared them. For example:

Excuses: They make excuses to why they aren't successful (none of which has to do with them). I understand that sometimes timing and demonic forces come against us to hinder us but we should never stop trying to execute the plans of God.

Procrastination: They are always coming up with a strategy (but that is as far as it goes); they lack the drive or motivation to work the vision.

Sabotage: They usually find a way that even when opportunity presents itself, it's torn down. They repeatedly find ways to not take full advantage of any prospect that may move them forward. They constantly look for the negative. They have resided in a place of negativity until the majority of their thoughts are negative.

"As a man thinketh within himself, so is he" Proverbs 23:7. Therefore, their thoughts become reality. The spirit of sabotage is so strong that it has the ability to blow holes in the solidity of a great opportunity. It's aimed directly at the foundation so that the opportunity slips through the cracks.

This is usually a cycle of actions that occur when progress is present. Therefore, there is a succession of events that occur to leave them in a place of "Nothing happens for me."

The sabotage doesn't always stop with themselves. They will make efforts to bring destruction to what others are doing (especially if the spirit of covetousness is intertwined in their hearts). Many times God releases their blessing in ways that they seem to miss.

I've seen it come and missed through their desire to do great things while despising humble beginnings or while trying to be successful at any cost. Occasionally the cost consists of using those around them to get ahead. They will begin doing something because someone close to them is doing it. They have lost sight of purpose for their lives and instead of spending that time with the Lord to get things back on track, they would rather just mimic what is working for someone else.

Motives always will separate light from darkness. Not that anything is wrong with doing great things, being successful, or doing what God has given you that looks familiar to what someone else is doing or has done. There has to be diversity. We must always do exactly what the Lord has purposed for us to do or what we are doing becomes a clone to another and vanity. Our divine purpose is the only area where we obtain the grace to flow and fulfill assignment.

Anger: They are angry with themselves, others, and sometimes even God. Others success is a constant reminder of how less fortunate than others they are.

When something great happens for others, it's never a release of genuine excitement for what God is doing in the lives of others. It's always what God hasn't done for "me".

If you have ever operated out of any of this, I can imagine this chapter being hard to read. I know because I too had to come to grips with the fact that I was once insecure. I didn't trust in the Lord enough that He would bring to pass those things He'd promised me.

I went through seasons of my life watching others walk in the very thing that God had promised me. I was living right and working for Him. Paying my tithes and sowing seeds faithfully. Yet nothing that I believed God for had manifested. In those seasons, I thought God had forgotten about me. I began to think God's will for my life was just that; to cause things to happen for others. This caused me to question was it worth it?

To go places and see lives changed by the working of ministry through me; yet come home to lack, sickness, and struggle for breakthrough. I would go to war in the spirit for people I didn't know personally and see yokes destroyed. However, they never reached back to say thank you or to sow a seed like they said, "the Lord told them to do."

I went through seasons of praying so hard for my family members and watching God pull them out. The very ones who I prayed for became the ones to harbor envy towards me and drag my name through the mud. Shortly after being revealed of their devices, the Lord instructed me to cover them. I spent so many nights in prayer and fasting for these individuals, that the nights turned into months.

I would be commissioned by God intercede without rest for my enemies subsequent to being advised of their plots towards me. God's heart would be moved with compassion towards them while I wondered if I would ever be vindicated. So I know about the Lord using these things to crush and kill anything that is in us that is not like Him. He desires for our hearts to remain pure and our hands to be clean at ALL times.

There were times when I had doubt, hurt, and insecurities in me. Constantly questioning if I was built to be the vessel that He designed to use in order to bring to pass what He said. I had to go to Him daily and constantly to pull forth a penetrable word of deliverance flowing from Heaven through my spirit (for me).

I needed Him to move in me while in this place. I would ask the Holy Spirit to provide me with the deposits that I would need in order to rout out all of my insecurities. I needed Him to create in me a clean heart and renew a right spirit so I could continue to walk in love.

There was a great desire awakened in me to be free from insecurities and the thoughts that held me bound. I wanted that sense of security in God that would have me unshakeable in my faith at all times. I began to seek Him for the true definition of who I was in Him. I found myself writing those things down to use as reference when those negative thoughts came to attack my mind and how I saw me.

 I truly believe that when we are highly concentrated with confidence it's because there is an underlining foundation of faith involved. As I began praying in the spirit, "building up my most holy faith" (Jude 1:20) God brought changes.

Through my experience, I now know a person who has confidence walks with the persona that "all things are possible for me", "I am just what I say I am", and "I can do this". These are the ones whom have listened to the voice that tells us that "ALL THINGS ARE POSSIBLE."

When you have been given an assignment that seems far beyond you; you cannot afford to listen to the voice of the enemy or the voice of insecurity. Totally believing what God says is essential. You have to make a conscious decision. Tell yourself, "I am going to break free, go for broke, and do all that I am purpose to do." God said it and I choose to believe "IT'S IN ME!"

Chapter IX
"Ready! Set! Go!"

Sometimes, it depends upon the nature of the mandate you may have to go alone. It would be nice to have a coach, Naomi, and a team of cheerleaders with you along the way. That's not always the case. However, the assignment continues.

We all are called with a purpose. God has created us with specifics in mind. It's for the glory of God. Why do we spend so much time trying to get the glory of man? What God has placed on the inside of us were never for that. It has to equip and assists man with necessary impartations for their journey into destiny. The glory belongs to God!

This means we are to give to them what we are required to give to them. Guess what? They may not even know what that is. God will always give us instructions before He releases us to them. So why do we act like we are ignorant? We go to them to see what we are supposed to give to them instead of doing what God has told us concerning them.

I can tell you many times I've missed Him by conversing with man about what I am to give to them. Originally, I go to them very confident that this is what I'm supposed to be doing. They tell me no, that's not it, through their actions. I reposition from what God has said usually to do nothing. Then when I am being corrected by the Lord I realized the very things they said no to; that's the impartation I was supposed to deposit into their lives. God has taught me to obey and leave the rest to Him. Quit permitting people through their words and deeds tell you what to impart.

If you are unsure go back to Him. He will guide you. They don't know if they are coming or going so don't rely on them for the answers. Neither do they know what God is doing to bring them into what they see.

So being Sovereign, he sends you. He sends you as revelation of HIS MIND. Now that you've encounter them you can't afford to forget what He said. Their breakthrough and sometimes lives depends upon you knowing and doing exactly what HE requires. Little distractions will come along the way. Make sure you find your stability in the Lord. I'm telling you, you can't always rely on man's response, reciprocation, or how they feel about you. If you rely on that you are going to get your feelings hurt and get off track. With most divine assignments, it's not about your relationship with the assignee. It's about their relationship with the Lord.

If you have insecurity, abandonment, or co-dependency issues, the enemy's is going to play that against you. There's no if or maybe's about it. It will happen.

Make sure that you allow the Lord to be the center. Those things that you desire from man find in the presence of the Lord. Search for that place in God where He is enough and stay there.

If not you will find yourself on an emotional rollercoaster, tangle up in soul ties, and this will make your assignment difficult to complete. Know that I am speaking from experience.

Chapter X
"Untie my Soul"

A soul tie is one of the worst entanglements a person can be caught up in. The original intent of the ties of the soul was for the glory of God. It was so the two would become one in love, heart, and spirit. The bible makes mention of souls being tied within the boundaries of marriage and friendship.

Nonetheless, when a person's soul is tied to another in any other form that takes them away from the perfect will of God it is ungodly. Soul ties in their divine context are built on a foundation of love and dedication. Yet, when you are in a relationship that takes you from a place of glory into a place of flesh gratification; it's demonic.

There are many stereotypes about soul ties that aren't true. Some seem to think you can only get a soul tie by sexual encounters. That's an untruth. There are emotional soul ties that are just as hard to recover from as sexual ones.

Men are drawn by what they see. The illusions (of what they see) are sometimes deceptive to the fulfillment of their absolute desire. In other words, a man maybe drawn by a woman's outer appearance but if there is something else about the woman that he dislikes he may be willing to compromise.

Depends on the man, he may look beyond his absolute desire being met for the pleasure of having a need met temporarily. He was attracted to her by her appearance which is common because men are fascinated by what they see. After they see what they desire they should inquire of the Lord. This is for their protection. Their desires ought to coincide with the perfect will of the Lord. If not what they thought was a common attraction could very well be a spirit of seduction.

The spirit of seduction has the power to lure you into things you wouldn't normally be attracted to. If you are uncovered and choose not to inquire of the Lord, it's a possibility that you will be lead off by it. Sadly, by the time the truth is reveal to you about that situation a tie is sown.

Deceptively thinking it was just a normal attraction, the enemy is making moves. He is going to try to set traps to get you tangled up and bound in your spirit.

The reality of the entanglement is that it
came to set you back and to get you off
course. Now your spirit is bind to another's
spirit. You feel the effects of it in your
minds, body, spirit, and soul. The soul tie
has grips on your full man. That's why it's
not easily shaken.

But ALL THINGS ARE POSSIBLE with
the Lord. The Blood of Jesus is powerful
and can sever any demonic hold. When you
come to the realization of what is happening
seek God for closure and until deliverance
occurs.

Women on the other hand are hearers. We
are drawn by what we hear. If it's what we
have heard God say or what we believe to be
truth for us we will roll with it. So, if a guy
comes to us and speaking our revealed truths
we are drawn to him by that.

Our attraction to him comes mostly by what
he speaks. That's why for us foreplay for
example happens long before physical
touching. If our mates have been affirming
us and building us up all week it's easier for
us to connect.

Women are drawn into emotional soul ties long before they are into physical. Maybe not in all cases but for the most part.

It's very important for men to affirm and build their mates. It keeps them protected in the relationship from her entering into an emotional tie with another man. Since that's how we are created to be drawn to men, that's what we need. We need conversation and we need to be affirmed by the ones we are with.

Even if you aren't a man that talks a lot learn to converse in a language that your mate understands. Give gifts. If you don't give gifts then find whatever it is that your woman needs from you and do that. Trust me when a man builds his woman he doesn't have to worry about her going outside of the relationship. It starts with what he says.

Now when what he says doesn't align with what he does. "Houston, there is a problem." We may give you the benefit of the doubt several times. We may not even make mention about how disappointed we are (for not making good on what was said) but we are thinking it! We will smile and move right along just to keep the peace.

SOMETIMES! Know there is a breaking point!

This is a dangerous place because there is a difference in men and women. Most women know their men. We are detectives by nature. We know when our mates are changing and something isn't right. We can sense it. Some call it women's intuition.

But men, listen," we hold a lot in." Although you may think your woman is very expressive with her lip service, I can guarantee she has held back at least 40 percent of her lip action.

Now getting back to the soul ties and how to prevent them from happening make sure you inquire of the Lord for direction in all things. If you have found yourself in the midst of a soul ties, repent for your actions, ask God to break it, and disconnect from that person.

You may not be able to break it all at once. Your deliverance may be a process. So little by little call, email, or text them not as much as usual. Try responding once a day, then that day will turn to once a week, a week will turn into once a month, and before you know it, you are free. But remember what is

tied in the spirit has to be untied in the spirit.
Amen! So go to God for your release and
move forward with HIM in the name of
Jesus.

Chapter XI
"Another Opportunity"

When an opportunity arises for us to forgive, alongside it comes an option to walk in pride. Pride brings delay and death to forgiveness. In pride, we tell ourselves, "We are so much better than others." Even in the midst of disagreements, it causes us to take the high rode. We become puffed up and refusal to apologize. Pride is an indication we have lost our positioning in God, which is humility.

"This is beneath me!" "There is nobody else doing it like me!" "I'm not dealing with them or this situation again." "They are not on my level!" These are some of the statements we make while walking in pride. I'm not saying that there won't be situations where we won't have to cut ties with people. But burning bridges shouldn't always be the primary option. If it is, it's time for us to discern our hearts.

The reasoning behind why the Lord connects us to people is not always to show our greatness, but to display HIS. Through our weakness, His Power is made perfect. This is found working through us in those times of humility. We underestimate the power of forgiveness. It truly walks hand and hand with love.

Forgiveness is a selfless expression of clemency towards others. In other words, we give them a pass. With this permit, we are saying, "I'm not going to hold you prisoner because of what happened between us!" It's a choice to love and release versus being revengeful.

Let me be clear, I'm not saying that just because we forgive someone that we should allow them "their" domicile back into our lives without discerning their intentions. Neither should we allow them to do harm to us. When I say harm I mean those things that caused injury to us initially or by any other way, form, or fashion. No! I'm NOT saying that at all.

I'm saying that when we forgive someone; it provides God the opportunity to forgive us. It allows us the opportunity to exercise love. Now if those who has injured us through time has proven to be trustworthy, repented, and has shown loyalty; we should be willing to start over.

I have learned that these experiences awaken discernment. Please believe, once we've been through some things keenness is activated and fully enforced. No matter where we are in life once we have grown through it, when it shows up, we recognize it.

Our keenness to a placed called "I've been here before" is a plus. Yet if we aren't aware, the enemy will use this as a place to build up walls. He will try to draw us into a place of our past and a place of defeat. Don't let him!

Know that when this alarm goes off in us, we will have a choice to make. Will I go with discernment? Or will I allow old issues to resurface (that will try to pull me into a place of insecurity)?

CHOOSE DISCERNMENT!!! It helps us to grow and mature. I truly believe the Lord allows us to have the discerning of spirits for our protection. We don't have to build walls from hurts and disappointments. As long as, we allow discernment to work in our lives there is no need for edgy issues of cynicism.

Discernment takes the place of having to go into a situation with the mindset of "Can I trust you?" It ushers us into a place of "I know exactly who and what I am dealing with."

Discerning of Spirits comes from the Holy Spirit. The Holy Spirit is fully aware, alive, and has knowledge of all things. When discernment is flowing through us, God takes us to a place of "NOTHING IS HIDDEN" and through the Spirit of the Lord, all things shall be revealed.

It doesn't matter if we see it in the lives of others; once we've lived through it we have valid keys. Those keys of wisdom becomes the very things someone one needs in order to experience breakthrough in their lives.

On the flipside, sometimes people do things out of ignorance and not with intentions of harming us. Though it hurts, if they have repented and turned from their foolish ways, we should grant them a pass to express their faithfulness.

Life will cause us to live with inner vows like "I'm not staying with a person who cheats on me" or "if they lie to me and I catch them, we can't be friends." I'm not saying that there's anything wrong with it. I'm just saying sometimes we need to handle every situation on an individual case basis.

That's like putting apples in a bowl. Some apples may rot before the other ones. More than likely that's going to happen. Now if you just take the apples that are still good and discard them with the bad ones where's the wisdom in that? Just like with that bowl of apples we should look at every situation carefully and find out what is suitable for us. Being patient enough to go through and put those things in proper perspective.

You do so by weighing the pros and cons. Once you have made your assessment, you will have the wisdom you need to make the right decisions.

Ask yourself: "Did they repent? Are they making a valid effort to make a mends? Can I trust them?" There's a saying we have here in the south. "Don't throw the baby out with the bath water!" In other words, learn how to keep what's of value and dispose of the rest. Now if they have proven to be an investment in your life overall, KEEP THEM!

Chapter XII
"Fight For It"

When you are having relational or marital issues, you can't trust everybody with your business. As friendly as someone maybe they will usually give you opinions more than likely according to the facts. In those times in your life, there's a requirement to go to the Lord strong in prayer.

Beyond popular demand that's not a time to do you, go back to the lifestyle you had in your single days, or give up without a fight. When you signed up for marriage in God's eyes the two were to become one.

God told me something very powerful, He said, "Tara how you treat Jason (my husband) will always reflects your relationship with me". In other words no matter how He treats me; I have the responsibility to always give him my best. It's my service unto the Lord.

Through ministering to many women about marriages, I decided to write this chapter in the book. There are times people are suffering in relationships or marriage and you want things back to the way they were when the affair began.

In order to do that, there has to be many changes. The change that you are after, I'm here to tell you begin in you. Reliance upon the nature of the issues determines the value of the cost that will be paid in order to see restoration. There is always a cost to having healthy relationships. You won't always have your way. Nonetheless, as you continue to sow the best of you, the best is what you will reap.

In my marriage, my husband and I have suffered many things including infidelity. We have had some heated fellowships that resulted to us being in two separate places. While we were separated after being hurt in church, hurting each other, and to create a better life for us (financially), I moved back to Mississippi and he stayed in Ohio to go to college. While there my husband had an affair.

God had revealed it to me previously in prayer but there is nothing like the blow of the worst being manifested in our lives. Nonetheless, through much prayer and fasting, we decided to salvage the marriage and move forward.

Today, our marriage is absolutely awesome! Sadly, it took all hell breaking loose to pull out the best in us. We realize our marriage is greater than the love we have for one another. It's built beyond what is tangible. IT'S FOR A GREATER PURPOSE WHICH IS THE GLORY OF GOD!

Yes, it was agonizing in the beginning. It was less painful to heal though because my husband was willing to come clean about his involvements with the other lady. I'm not saying we were parlaying in the park but the honesty helped build up walls of trust again.

We begin to spend much time alone in prayer and together really seeking the Lord for direction. Let me mention, upon learning of the affair we had agreed to divorce and go our separate ways. We cried together about the thought of divorcing but looking at our situation it seemed hopeless.

We had no clue on how we could make it through everything that we were facing at that time. We went to pastors and they prayed for us. It was SOLEMNLY God who brought restoration to us through those individuals who stood with us and our willingness to surrender our will to HIS WILL.

Getting back to what I was saying if you are having marital issues and you desire to salvage your marriage, start giving the best to your spouse before the Lord. Be willing to do it unto the Lord, even without results. Let me say you may not see any immediate results from your actions. Keep at it God will honor you!!!

I didn't at the outset see the results I wanted but I kept pray and speaking what the Lord said concerning my marriage. We have many prophecies on CD. I would play those in my car on my way to work. This gave me a foundational place to always go back to when I would battle internally. (Note: After going weeks without any changes, you will war in your mind if what you are doing is working. Keep going)

While we were separated, I would only talk to him about the kids. Not pressuring him or questioning him about his where about. I needed to stay focus on the overall results. When God would show me something, I would go back to God with what He released. I learned early off, Jason didn't need to hear about what God was showing me. It was for me.

He was in a battle of his own and it would only lead us into differences. So, as the Lord would allow it to unfold before me, I would pray and speak the word.

Little by little, things begin to turn. I changed as well. So if you are experiencing this, know no matter how bad your situation looks God can turn it! You just have to fight for it!!!!

Chapter XIII
"Choose Love"

When you find someone who loves you cherish that. Don't get relaxed thinking the battle is won. Do those same things that you did before, when you were on the chase. Pursue them with Love! As you follow Him, He will give you what you need to effortlessly release love into the lives of those associated to you. God will allow the love you have towards them to grow to the point it covers their entire atmosphere.

They should never have to question if you really love them. Your actions will speak for you. Love has a way when it's effective to birth reciprocity. So never, get caught in a self- seeking release. There are many types of love:

Eros Love is *physical passion, gratification, and fulfillment. It is inferred in many scriptures and is the only kind of love that God restricts to a one-man and one-woman relationship within the bounds of marriage* (Heb. 13:4; 1 Cor. 7:25; Eph. 5:31).

Storge Love - *is the natural bond and expressed affection between mother and infant, father, children, and kin.*

Phileo Love - *is a love of the affections. It is delighting to be in the presence of another, a warm feeling that comes and goes with intensity. The Bible encourages it but it is never a direct command. This type of love is based on the feelings. God Himself operated in agape love towards us.*

Agape Love - *Agape love is God's kind of love. It is seeking the welfare and betterment of another regardless of how we feel. Agape does not have the primary meaning of feelings or affection. Jesus made the greatest display of it when he went to the cross and died for us regardless of how He felt.*

By the time, we meet people unless they are our children they have experienced all kinds of things. Love is a force that helps to heal and mend brokenness. When we are blessed to find someone who loves us it's like a breath of fresh air. We want to do more. Love enables us to spread our wings and fly high.

So, when you find someone who absolutely adores you receive and interchange that. I'm not oblivious to the fact that some people love is tainted. They have no clue fouled by fleshly views of what love is and what it looks like. Flee from those (especially if they don't want to be free).

I can recall being involved with a guy who I cared for. Early in the relationship he started showing "crazy" tendencies. He wanted to know where I was at all times. Every disagreement we would have, he literally wanted to drive to a pond or creek and jump in.

I said, Lord you are going to have to help me get out of this. I would avoid him thinking he would get the picture. He would cut his wrist and all sorts of irrational things.

I prayed for the Lord to remove him without him being of any harm to me. He eventually fell for another woman talking about celebration. Hallelujah for my way of escape!!!!

Choose love! One that is divine and not self-seeking, selfish, or tainted. When you find that love don't give up on it. No matter what when it's love you can weather any storm.

Every healthy relationship has differences. What makes it healthy is you acquire to work through those variances together. You remain devoted.

It's an awesome feeling knowing someone has your back and best interest in mind. Love is truly a powerful force. Even if you have been injured in love, don't allow what another person has done keep you from receiving a love that is real. Your healing is tied to it.

When someone truly loves you, never make him or her compensate for what happened in your past. You owe it them to return that love back. Be obliged for liberty and that love has yet again found you. Choose love.

Chapter XIV
"YOU"

God is longings to have an intimate relationship with us. He yearns for a relationship that is not dysfunctional. Every time we handle matters on our own or consult man before or more than Him, it hinders us.

Our relationship with Him is scarred by our inabilities to trust him. Therefore, we suffer. He says, "In our weakness His power is made perfect." If we are constantly taking our issues elsewhere, it has the same effect as us going outside of our natural relationships for fulfillment. We are therefore saying to Him, His power is not made perfect in our weakness. He is not enough.

God uses circumstances and situations to show us who we are, where we are, and how much we need Him. It's funny how we fail to see it as it is. We look at situations and use them as an opportunity to place blame on others.

Circumstances come to develop us. Instead of saying, who they are and what they have done to wrong us; we should see how we have erred in trusting so many things over Him.

Rather than placing the blame on others, we must learn to take responsibility for our actions. Trust me; I know it will take discipline. We all look for that person in the natural we can count on. I've learned, the more I take my concerns to the Lord and have fellowship with the Him; the more visible He becomes.

God is kind. He is not the type to go where He isn't wanted. Who do you know in the natural wants to be the person everyone goes to when they are in trouble? No one! So He is seemingly less visible because of the time we put in with Him. The more we spend in His presence; the more HE REVEALS of HIMSELF.

He is masked through all the many things we put before Him. We end up, just narrowing Him down to be the "go to" God and our "pusher". I won't stay here long but God is more than one who gives us our weekly high. He is more than a three times a month "quickie". He is absolutely more than any desire or manifestation thereof.

He wants to be our all in all every day of the week. And not just some God that we perform for just to get our needs met. He desires intimacy. So that when things occur he can warn and give us instructions before we need them.

Our relationship, when it's in its proper context will keep us wanting to spend time with Him and not just for what He has to offer. Some things are ignited and we reciprocate to Him the best of us.

Today, the heart of God cries for a man who is after His heart not His hand. When we become the ones who goes wholeheartedly after His heart He easily releases what's in His hand.

Ultimately
"A letter to you"

Greeting Readers,

I pray that through this book you have received something that will help you handle these situations if they were to arise. Know that no matter what you are in and are called to; the Lord has great things in store for you.

Never conform to what you experience but be transformed by the renewing of you mind in Christ Jesus. There are no limits or boundaries in God. So don't limit Him in your expectations. All things are possible.

You just have to simply believe! Pursue your dreams! Is there anything too hard for God? I think not!!!!! Thanks for your support and may the Lord continually manifest Himself daily in your lives. Be encouraged! "If the Lord be for you who can be against you? I mean really?"

In His service,

Tara Walker Smith